ALL ABOUT I_____

MY NAME IS...

MY AGE

MY BIRTHDAY

MY PET

MY FAVORITE COLOR

MY FAVORITE FOOD

I REALLY LIKE...

Positive Affirmation
Handwriting Practice

I am strong, inside
and out.

Practice Time!

Positive Affirmation Handwriting Practice

Making mistakes

helps me grow and

learn new things.

Practice Time!

Positive Affirmation
Handwriting Practice

I am unique and that
makes me special.

Practice Time!

Name: _____   Date: _____

Positive Affirmation
Handwriting Practice

I can handle
whatever comes my
way.

Practice Time!

Name: _____ Date: _____

Positive Affirmation
Handwriting Practice

I get better and
learn new things
every day.

Practice Time!

Positive Affirmation
Handwriting Practice

I can try something
again, even if I fail
the first time.

Practice Time!

Name: _____   Date: _____

Positive Affirmation
Handwriting Practice

I am loved by my
family and friends.

Practice Time!

Name: _____   Date: _____

Positive Affirmation
Handwriting Practice

I can challenge my
brain and learn new
things.

Practice Time!

Positive Affirmation
Handwriting Practice

I am kind to myself
and others.

Practice Time!

Name: _____   Date: _____

Positive Affirmation
Handwriting Practice

I am brave because
I can take on new
challenges.

Practice Time!

_____

- -

_____

- -

_____

- -

_____

Positive Affirmation
Handwriting Practice

I believe in my
abilities.

Practice Time!

Positive Affirmation
Handwriting Practice

I can take a deep
breath and try
again.

Practice Time!

Positive Affirmation
Handwriting Practice

I am capable of
learning new things.

Practice Time!

Positive Affirmation
Handwriting Practice

I am beautiful and
unique just the way
I am.

Practice Time!

Positive Affirmation
Handwriting Practice

I am brave and can
face my fears.

Practice Time!

Positive Affirmation
Handwriting Practice

Every day is a day
to learn something
new!

Practice Time!

_____

- -

_____

- -

_____

- -

_____

- -

_____

Positive Affirmation
Handwriting Practice

I choose to be
happy and find joy
every day.

Practice Time!

Positive Affirmation
Handwriting Practice

I can be a good
friend and a leader
today.

Practice Time!

Name: _____   Date: _____

Positive Affirmation
Handwriting Practice

I am responsible
for my own
happiness.

Practice Time!

Positive Affirmation
Handwriting Practice

I am a good friend
and make others
feel good too.

Practice Time!

Positive Affirmation
Handwriting Practice

I am grateful for
all the good things
in my life.

Practice Time!

Name: _____   Date: _____

Positive Affirmation
Handwriting Practice

I can always ask
for help when I
need it.

Practice Time!

_____

_____

_____

_____

Positive Affirmation
Handwriting Practice

I am getting better
at solving problems.

Practice Time!

Name: _____ Date: _____

Positive Affirmation
Handwriting Practice

I am creative and
can think of fun
ideas.

Practice Time!

Positive Affirmation
Handwriting Practice

I am patient, and
good things take
time.

Practice Time!

_____

- -

_____

- -

_____

- -

_____

Name: _____   Date: _____

Positive Affirmation
Handwriting Practice

I am a good listener
and understand
others.

Practice Time!

Positive Affirmation
Handwriting Practice

I am important and
have a purpose in
this world.

Practice Time!

_____

- -

_____

- -

_____

- -

_____

- -

_____

Positive Affirmation
Handwriting Practice

I am full of energy
and ready to
explore.

Practice Time!

Positive Affirmation
Handwriting Practice

I am loved for

being exactly who I

am.

Practice Time!

Name: _____   Date: _____

Positive Affirmation
Handwriting Practice

I am safe, and
everything will be
ok.

Practice Time!

Positive Affirmation
Handwriting Practice

I am confident in
myself and my
choices.

Practice Time!

_____

- -

_____

- -

_____

- -

_____

Positive Affirmation
Handwriting Practice

I am a good
learner, and love to
discover new things.

Practice Time!

_____

- -

_____

- -

_____

- -

_____

- -

_____

Positive Affirmation
Handwriting Practice

I am a positive

thinker and see the

bright side of life.

Practice Time!

Name: _____ Date: _____

Positive Affirmation
Handwriting Practice

I am a helper and
can make a
difference.

Practice Time!

Positive Affirmation
Handwriting Practice

I am curious and
love to learn new
things.

Practice Time!

Positive Affirmation
Handwriting Practice

I am surrounded by
love and support.

Practice Time!

Positive Affirmation
Handwriting Practice

I am responsible
for my own actions.

Practice Time!

_____

_____

_____

_____

_____

_____

Positive Affirmation
Handwriting Practice

I am loved just the
way I am.

Practice Time!

Made in the USA
Columbia, SC
11 March 2024

32483507R00022